# CURIOUS
## questions &
## answers about...

# The Solar System

You live in our curious Solar System too, and we want to find out about YOU!

What's your NAME?

How OLD are you?

What's the first thing you'd pack for a trip to outer space?

First published in 2018 by Miles Kelly Publishing Ltd
Harding's Barn, Bardfield End Green, Thaxted, Essex, CM6 3PX, UK

Copyright © Miles Kelly Publishing Ltd 2018

This edition printed 2019

2 4 6 8 10 9 7 5 3 1

Publishing Director  Belinda Gallagher

Creative Director  Jo Cowan

Editorial Director  Rosie Neave

Design Manager  Simon Lee

Image Manager  Liberty Newton

Production  Elizabeth Collins, Jennifer Brunwin-Jones

Reprographics  Stephan Davis, Callum Ratcliffe-Bingham

Assets  Lorraine King

ISBN 978-1-78989-044-0

Printed in China

British Library Cataloguing-in-Publication Data
A catalogue record for this book is available from the British Library

Made with paper from a sustainable forest

www.mileskelly.net

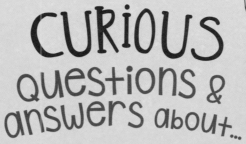

# CURIOUS
## Questions & answers about...
# The Solar System

Words by Ian Graham

Illustrations by Barbara Bakos

MILES KELLY

# Where is the Solar System?

It's all around you. The Solar System is the Sun, eight planets and everything else that moves through space with the Sun.

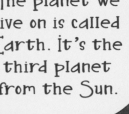

The planet we live on is called Earth. It's the third planet from the Sun.

## Sun
In the middle of the Solar System is a star called the Sun.

## Earth

## Venus

## Mercury

## Planets
Planets are the giant things like the Earth that travel round the Sun. There are eight in our Solar System.

The four planets closest to the Sun are small worlds made mostly of rock.

## Moons

A moon is a small world that circles bigger object – usually a planet. Earth has one, and is made of rock.

Mars

Zoooom!

Saturn

The four planets farthest from the Sun are giant balls of gas and liquid.

Uranus

Asteroid Belt

Jupiter

Neptune

Asteroids

Asteroids are rocky worlds smaller than planets. There are millions of them.

Dwarf planets

Similar to planets in many ways, dwarf planets go round the Sun, but are not as big as planets.

5

# How do you make a solar system?

Our Solar System began as a huge cloud of gas and dust in space.

① 

Dust and gas →

How did the Solar System begin, and where did it come from?

First, an exploding star pushed against the cloud. The whole dusty cloud began to shrink.

③

So, there was a swirling disc of dust and gas — then what happened?

The dust and gas began to stick together, forming lumps that smashed into each other.

Lumps

② Whoosh!

Flat disc

Why is the Solar System flat, like a plate?

As the cloud got smaller, it started to spin. Spinning flattened it out into a wide, thin disc.

④ How did the lumpy disc become the Sun and planets?

Planets

Sun

Huge energy built up in the centre of the disc, causing the lump in the middle to become the Sun. The biggest other lumps formed the planets.

# Is the Sun hotter than an oven?

The Sun's surface is over 20 times hotter than a regular oven! The centre is even hotter – thousands of times hotter than an oven. It would melt the oven!

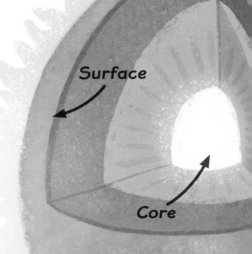

Surface

Core

NEVER NEVER look at the Sun. It's so bright and hot that it will hurt your eyes.

## What is the Sun made of?

It's mostly made of stuff called hydrogen and helium. On Earth, hydrogen and helium are gases.

HYDROGEN

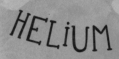

HELIUM

## Why is the Sun bigger than other stars?

It isn't – the Sun is actually a small star. It looks much bigger than the other stars you see at night, because it is much closer to Earth than those other stars. They're all suns, but they are very far away.

> Side-by-side with another star, I'm actually pretty tiny!

> Scientists have found some suns that are 100 times bigger than the one in the Solar System!

## Will the Sun be there forever?

> No, but don't worry – it isn't going to disappear any time soon. The Sun should be there for another 5000 million years.

# Where does the Sun go at night?

The Sun doesn't go anywhere – it's the Earth that is moving!

This spinning motion makes it look to us on Earth as if the Sun rises in the morning, crosses the sky, and then disappears at sunset.

Our planet spins around an invisible line called the axis. It's daytime for you when the side you live on faces the Sun.

Axis

N

Light rays

S

Sunset

## Why is a day 24 hours long?

It takes 24 hours for Earth to spin around once, and we call this a day.

# Why do we have seasons?

Because Earth's axis is tilted. This means different bits of Earth get the Sun's direct rays at different times during Earth's orbit (journey around the Sun).

## What is the Equator?

It's an invisible line that circles Earth. It divides it into a northern (top) half and southern (bottom) half.

Equator

In June, it's summer in the north and winter in the south.

In March, it's spring in the north, and autumn in the south.

In December, it's winter in the north and summer in the south.

In September, it's autumn in the north and spring in the south.

## What is a year?

A year is the time it takes for the Earth to complete one orbit of the Sun.

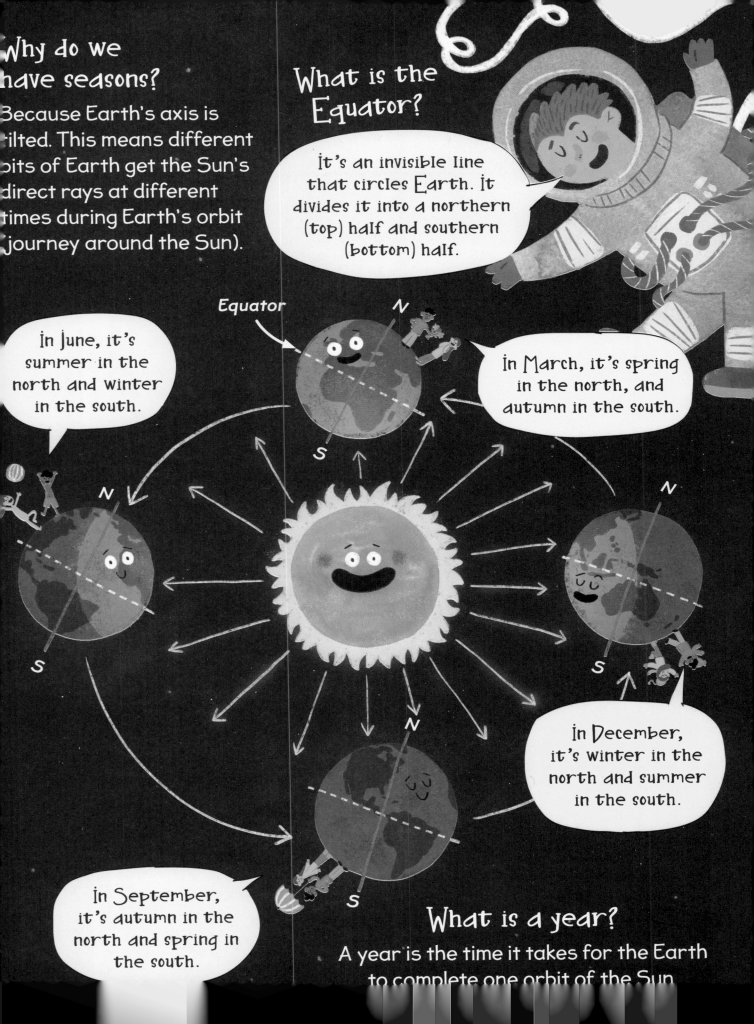

# Did you know?

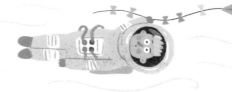

**Jupiter** has a huge storm called the Great Red Spot – it's about three times bigger than **Earth**.

Neptune is the Solar System's windiest planet, with winds ten times faster than the worst hurricanes on **Earth**.

**Saturn** is famous for its rings, but **Jupiter**, **Uranus** and **Neptune** have them too.

My rings are easy to see, because they're made of pieces of ice. Sunlight bounces off the ice and lights them up.

Our rings are thin, dark and dusty so they're hard to see.

The centre of the **Earth** is made of metal so hot that some of it has melted and turned to liquid.

You can jump six times higher on the **Moon** than you can on **Earth**.

Jupiter's moon **Ganymede** is the biggest moon in the Solar System – even bigger than the planet **Mercury**.

Dust storms are common on **Mars**. The sky there is pinky red, as so much red dust is blown about by the wind.

If you know where to look, you can see five planets without a telescope – **Mercury**, **Venus**, **Mars**, **Jupiter** and **Saturn**.

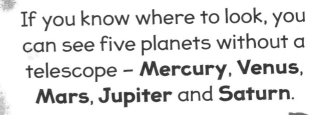

They are so far away they look like stars.

I'm only about half the width of the USA!

Astronauts who visited the **Moon** brought 382 kilograms of Moon rocks back with them.

**Pluto** was the Solar System's ninth planet – until 2006 when scientists decided to call it a dwarf planet instead.

There are between two and five solar eclipses every year.

Giant **Jupiter** spins so fast it has the shortest day of any planet – just 9 hours 55 minutes.

A solar eclipse happens when the **Moon** passes in front of the **Sun**. The Moon's shadow then moves across **Earth**, causing darkness to fall.

# Are other planets like Earth?

Earth and the other three planets closest to the Sun are alike in some ways, but no other planet is exactly like Earth.

**Why is it always so hot here?**

Mercury is very hot because it's the closest planet to the Sun. It's smaller than Earth and it looks like the Moon.

Mercury

**Why am i known as Earth's twin planet?**

Venus

Venus and Earth are similar in size and structure – but the two planets look very different. Venus is wrapped in thick clouds of acid. They trap heat, so Venus is even hotter than Mercury.

Earth

Why am i blue?

Water covers 70 percent of Earth's surface. Sunlight contains all the colours of the rainbow. When sunlight shines on Earth, the water reflects the blue part of the light back into space.

Mars

Why am i called the Red Planet?

Mars is a small world about half the size of Earth. It looks red all over because its soil and rocks are full of rusty iron. Mars is a rusty planet.

# What are the outer planets like?

The four planets farthest from the Sun – Jupiter, Saturn, Uranus and Neptune – couldn't be more different from Earth. They are giant worlds made of gas and liquid.

Where did my rings come from?

Jupiter

How big am I?

Saturn

Jupiter is the biggest planet in the Solar System. It's so big that more than a thousand Earths would fit inside it!

Uranus

What's special about me?

No one knows. They might have come from an icy moon that broke up ...

... or they might be ice left over from making Saturn.

This blue-green gassy world was the first planet ever to be found by someone looking through a telescope. It was discovered in 1781 by a man called William Herschel (1738–1822), who became famous overnight as a result.

What am I made of?

Neptune

Both Uranus and Neptune are made mostly of water, ammonia and methane, and it's the methane that gives them their blue colour. Jupiter and Saturn are made mostly of hydrogen and helium, like the Sun.

# Do planets ever crash into each other?

Almost never. Billions of years ago, a planet the size of Mars crashed into Earth and sent lots of rock flying out into space. Can you guess what happened next?

① A planet called Theia crashed into Earth.

② The crash threw lots of rocks into space around Earth.

③ The rocks in space came together and became the Moon.

The Moon is the only place beyond Earth that humans have set foot on.

# What's it like on the Moon?

The Moon is very dry and covered with grey dust. There are mountains, but there is no air, and the sky is always inky black.

# Why is the Moon covered with craters?

These dents are made when rocks flying through space hit the Moon.

④ The Moon travels through space at a distance of 384,400 kilometres from Earth. Every year the Moon moves 4 centimetres further away from Earth.

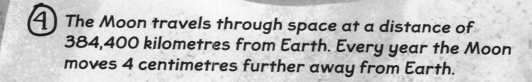

# Would you rather?

Would you rather discover a new planet, like **William Herschel** did...

...or work out that all the planets in the Solar System orbit the Sun, like **Nicolaus Copernicus** did?

Would you rather live on **Earth** for your whole life, or spend your whole life in a **space station** where you could float about weightless?

Would you rather kick a ball really far on the **Moon** or make a red sandcastle on **Mars**?

If I lived on Mercury I'd be sixteen!

If I lived on Neptune I'd be younger than you!

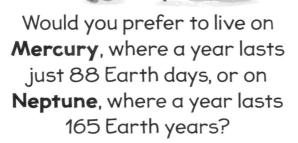

Would you prefer to live on **Mercury**, where a year lasts just 88 Earth days, or on **Neptune**, where a year lasts 165 Earth years?

Which part of astronaut training would you rather do:

Work in a huge tank of water to practise **space walks**...

...or take a spin to get a feel for **extreme forces**?

If you had to name a new planet, would you rather call it **Aether**, after the Greek god of light, or **Erebus**, the god of darkness?

On a space mission, would you rather be the **pilot** flying the spacecraft, or a **specialist**, doing experiments and going on space walks?

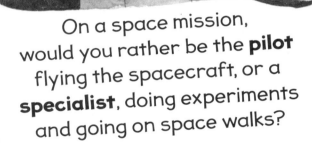

Would you rather live on Uranus in **winter**, when the Sun doesn't rise for 20 years, or in **summer**, when it doesn't set for 20 years?

Would you rather slow down **Earth's** spin so days are longer, or move Earth closer to the **Sun** so that the weather is warmer?

# What are shooting stars?

They're not stars! They're small pieces of rock that fly through space and into the air around Earth. Rubbing against the air heats them until they glow. They are also called meteors.

When lots of meteors appear in the sky, it's called a meteor shower.

## Where do shooting stars go?

The smallest burn up and disappear. Others sometimes fall all the way down to the ground. If they land on Earth, they're called meteorites.

## What happens when a big meteorite hits Earth?

It makes a hole in the ground called a crater. A famous crater in Arizona, USA, was made by a meteorite 50 metres across that hit the ground 50,000 years ago.

Comets are like giant dusty snowballs in space. If they fly near the Sun, some of the ice turns to gas and bursts out, carrying dust with it. The dust forms a tail that is lit up by sunlight.

## How big are space rocks?

The biggest rocks in space are asteroids. Some can be up to 1000 kilometres across. Most asteroids are found in the Asteroid Belt between Mars and Jupiter.

**-200°** Celsius.

*Brrrrrrrrrr!*

The average temperature on the Solar System's coldest planet, Neptune.

**178** moons have been found going around planets so far. More might be found in future.

Life appeared on Earth about **4,000,000,000** years ago.

**7,500,000,000**: The number of people living on Earth.

**0**

The number of moons that the planets Mercury and Venus have.

The Solar System is about **4,600,000,000** years old.

The Solar System's tallest mountain is Olympus Mons on Mars. It's nearly **3** times the height of the tallest mountain on Earth, Mount Everest.

How many astronauts have walked on the Moon?

**12**

The Sun is so big that **109** Earths would fit side by side across its middle.

**150 million** kilometres: the distance from Earth to the Sun.

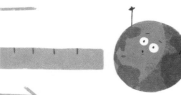

Halley's Comet appears in the sky every

**76**

years.

Just over **8** minutes: the amount of time it takes for sunlight to reach Earth.

**165**

The number of Earth years it takes the farthest planet, Neptune, to go once around the Sun.

**3**

...the number of days it takes astronauts to fly to the Moon in a spacecraft.

There are **5** dwarf planets in the Solar System. They are called...

Eris     Pluto     Haumea    Makemake   Ceres

# How do we know about other planets?

No human has ever visited another planet, but we learn about them by sending robot spacecraft to study them. We have sent more spacecraft to Mars than any other planet.

*Solar panels provide power*

*Robotic arm*

I used my robotic arm to scoop up Martian soil to find out what it's made of.

Phoenix lander

## Do spacecraft land on other planets?

Yes! Spacecraft that land on a planet are called landers. They take photographs of the surface and measure things like the temperature and wind speed. A spacecraft called Phoenix landed on Mars in 2008.

Mars Reconnaissance Orbiter

Powerful camera

How do we get good photos of Mars?

Robot spacecraft like me are called orbiters. We fly round and round it, like tiny moons. As we circle, we take photos and send them back to Earth by radio.

## What is a rover?

Some of the spacecraft on Mars have wheels so that they can move around and explore more of the planet. They're called rovers. A rover called Curiosity landed on Mars in 2012.

My mission is to investigate Martian climate and geology, to find out whether Mars can support any life.

Special instruments measure temperatures, wind speeds, radiation, and much more

Curiosity

# Is there life anywhere else?

Not that we know of – the search goes on. The spacecraft we have sent to other planets have been searching for signs of life there.

Erm... hello? Is anyone at home?

## Why is there life on Earth?

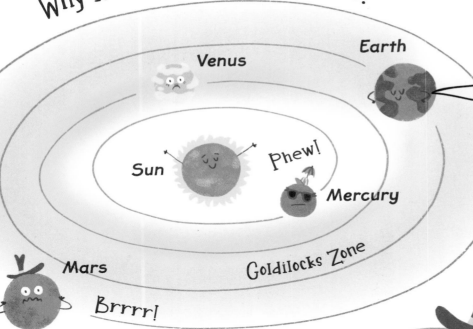

Venus

Earth

Sun

Phew!

Mercury

Mars

Goldilocks Zone

Brrrr!

My distance from the Sun means I have light, water and the correct temperature for life. I'm in what's called the 'Goldilocks Zone' – it's just right.

## Why did people think aliens lived on Mars?

When people first used telescopes to study Mars they thought they saw lines on its surface. The idea spread that these were canals, made by aliens.

When spacecraft visited Mars, they found a dry, dusty planet with no cana– or aliens.

# Is there water anywhere else in the Solar System?

Scientists think there may be oceans beneath the surfaces of some of Jupiter and Saturn's icy moons. Future missions will search for life there.

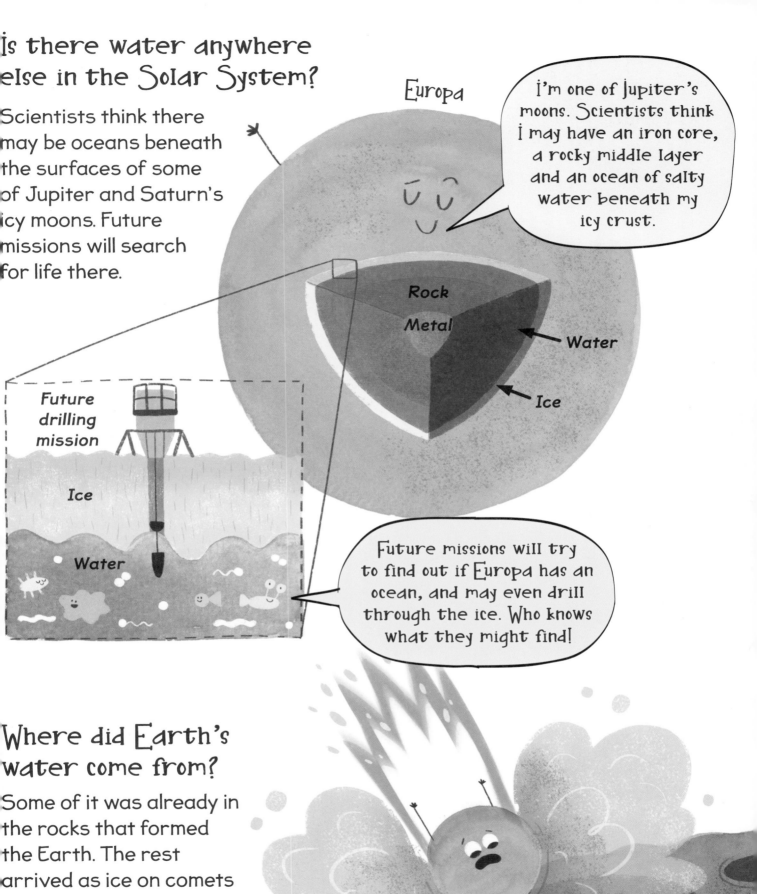

Europa

I'm one of Jupiter's moons. Scientists think I may have an iron core, a rocky middle layer and an ocean of salty water beneath my icy crust.

Rock

Metal

Water

Ice

*Future drilling mission*

Ice

Water

Future missions will try to find out if Europa has an ocean, and may even drill through the ice. Who knows what they might find!

# Where did Earth's water come from?

Some of it was already in the rocks that formed the Earth. The rest arrived as ice on comets and other space rocks that crashed into Earth soon after it formed.

# A compendium of questions

## Why aren't planets square?

Planets are round because of gravity. This special force pulls everything inwards, forming a ball shape.

## Why is Earth called Earth?

It comes from an ancient word meaning land. Earth is the only planet that wasn't named after an ancient Greek or Roman god.

## Where is the best view of the Sun?

Standing on Mercury when it is at its closest to the Sun, the Sun would appear more than three times as large as it does from Earth.

## Which moon is the weirdest?

Hmmm... maybe Saturn's moon Enceladus. It spews jets of gas and ice from its south pole!

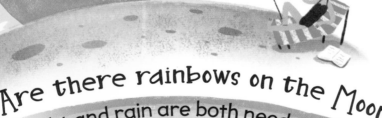

## Are there rainbows on the Moon?

Sunlight and rain are both needed for a rainbow. There is no rain on the Moon, so you will never see a rainbow there.

## Why is the Earth's sky blue?

As sunlight travels through air, the blue part of the light is scattered in all directions, so the sky looks blue.

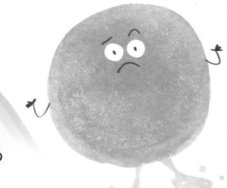

# Can a spacecraft land on a gas planet?

No – and they can't fly through them either! The extreme temperature and pressure inside would crush a spacecraft.

# When did the first spacecraft go to the Moon?

In 1959, Luna 2 became the first spacecraft to crash-land there – no astronauts were onboard.

# Is there lightning on other planets?

Yes. Spacecraft have seen lightning storms on Venus, Jupiter and Saturn.

# Who is the Man in the Moon?

Some people think marks on the surface look like a face. Others think they can see the shape of a rabbit.

# Are all the stars part of our Solar System?

No – the Sun is our only star. All the others are outside our Solar System.

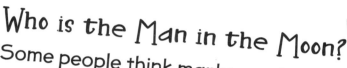

Many other stars have their own families of planets.

Mercury  Venus  Earth  Mars

Jupiter  Saturn  Uranus  Neptune

# Why are the planets different colours?

Because planets are made of different mixtures of rocks and gases that reflect light in different ways.